Forever's

Brett Harrison

Copyright 2016 Brett Harrison
All Rights Reserved

For more from Brett Harrison, check out
www.facebook.com/brettharrisonauthor
and
www.slurryartistemporium.com
or
purchase his books on Amazon
(Brett Harrison Mysteries are from a different author and unrelated)

Contents

Dag Hammershold Markings (upstairs escape)......................... 5
Roses in the Snow... 6
straddling myself naked in the pottery studio at night (nonsexual).......... 7
sweet idiot wind... 10
If I Die Early and Mean.. 11
Steer The Stars.. 12
suction cup opera.. 13
StarShine Lady... 14
oceans and acid.. 15
the river shivers (sadistic beercan)............................. 16
Violet Stereo.. 17
when so many things are wrong.................................... 18
8-18-'15... 20
anemic moon and rock explosions.................................. 21
On The Decline... 22
Bad Stuff Is Temporary... 23
Black and Green.. 24
Chinese New Year... 25
Dear Sex-Slave Masters (A Poem of Cosmic Redemption)............. 26
Dreaming Slurpid... 28
Forever's Crushing Dawn.. 29
Found my song.. 30
Free As The Sky Is Wide.. 32
Grungy Tenement in Heaven.. 33
Hot-Air Balloons... 34
Infinite Imagination's Rebirth................................... 35
little stars and little prayers a go-go.......................... 36
Living Profound.. 37
Markus Means/Jesus' Joke/but roll................................ 38
Masterpiece Crescendo 1 & 2...................................... 39
mesmerizing Timeless cascades:................................... 40
My Brother, I Wonder... 41
my soul's song of love... 42
mystery's door... 43
onward... 44
ouroboric.. 45
Pharaoh Dance.. 46
Portal Soul.. 47

Rocking in the Heart	49
rolling jelly	50
The Joyous Answer (2)	51
Sacrificial Columns	53
SunThruJoyousTears Images	54
somewhere in snapping keys	55
splendid excellence chiseling dance	56
Staring Out	57
Starry Skies, Momma's Eyes	59
stars and balls and happy monkeys	60
About the Author:	61

Dag Hammershold Markings (upstairs escape)

Liquid language languidly lasts
in my asymmetrical retinal play
disparities dance, love in a glance
and identity peels away.

i pry a moment into nothing.
i pry a crowbar into my brain
i pry a snapshot into an apocalyptic plane
i pry a smile apart,
and hide in my upstairs escape.
i am Brett, ashamed as can be.

trying to escape
but too afraid of every door
young baby brett
wanders through his delirium life
thinking the sky is his floor

3-15-06/1-22-06/12-3-2008

Roses in the Snow
1-1-14

And I'm sad and I'm scared
And I'm hopeful and I'm joyous
All wrapped up in a warm chalice flame—
And I would stand on a mountain,
And I would call her name
If the world didn't always
beat me down again.

And I'm drowning with tears
yet soaring like an eagle,
for I'm brave enough to believe now
that it can come true...
And I'm lighting candles to illuminate
my whole wide world
and I'm beginning to feel
I can sing from my mountain,
I can sing her reverent name
and the earth will grow
into smiles and roses in the snow.

and so here's to the answer,
that it was finally found
and here's to her grace and her glory,
that our love will forever abound.

Thank you Heaven and thank you Light
Thank you song that's made it right
Thank you Soul that grows and sings
Thank you Becca, and thank you again.

straddling myself naked in the pottery studio at night (nonsexual)

9-25-2014

again, my country went to war,
1st world against 3rd world,
rich against poor,
the anger of the inadequacy of money's supremacy
against the anger of those misused and abused by money's attempt
at supremacy
while babies die,
and both sides turn evil.

i straddle myself naked in the pottery studio
thinking of the idiocy of war
the idiocy of the thought that we can murder badness,
that two wrongs, multiplied millionsfold, can make a right,
when a terrorist wouldn't be if we hadn't supported
the torture of his dad, the rape of his mother, the subjugation of his country,
so that we can afford cheaper shit.

i see my sins, splayed out before me
my anger, so severe; my insanity, so incredible,
writing dire words to my mother of her sins,
becoming so angry at my father for his
that i attempted to write him the biggest bitchslap
but was made sick and ill by the power of my anger,
unable to complete the ginormous thought,

i thought of my true love, who my rational brain believes hates me,
our love, which was cursed for unknown reasons,
made impossible, and tortured, despite our best intentions,
despite the blessings of God, of limitless audacity,
of absolute, reverent, mutual, awe-filled recognition,
and six years later, the curse has turned us both unforgiveable,
and though God renders us still beautiful in the eyes of each other and so many others,
still we are too afraid of ourselves to face the other,

i saw my future, a tumbling mass of anger rolling down hills,
bombarding towns like a villainous nuclear mudslide,
my friends and family turning against me
disgusted by who I had become, and Me,
so certain that by fighting my endless crucifixion,
by crucifying back,
I was sending them God's judgment that would purify them,
purification through flame,
as I grow more agonized, less able to eat,

more tortured by the day,
and my innocence dissolves and is replaced by the acid
the acid of contempt

"but this is what it is to be a man."

rolling with the realization of my power, my evil,
having thought that "no pain, no gain" to justify

i throw clothes on, walk outside the studio to pee in the desert dirt,
beneath the cool night air,
and hear in my head Yoda's words
"Anger, Fear, Aggression: The dark side of the force are they." Anger. My sin.

And suddenly I understand anger.
Anger is pushing guilt onto another,
guilt is domination through obligation,
through debt
justified by pain, anger is its own insane justification

and so, yes, Christ was true, was right, was Good
forgiveness is Anger's cure, and in the face of the injustice,
greed, domination and destruction of the evil,
forgiveness is the audacity of loving them anyway,
for to know a soul's whole story is to love it,
confusion and ignorance which consumes them and all,

for we are all with me, straddling ourselves naked in this pottery studio
praying for forgiveness
and finally beginning to realize that we can be forgiveness

loving life and earth and pain,
destruction and all,
while still ferocious working to resolve the problem,

with unwavering love and resolve and bravery,
for forgiveness turns the world to love,
and this is the challenge of our times
that determines whether babies will starve or thrive.

so

so never shall i give in to anger again,
but resolve again to love and forgive,
the flies that harass and bite me,
those angry at me whose anger is like violence against me, punching me,

for the road to hell is paved with good intentions,

but to sacrifice one moral one time for a "higher good"
to murder a murderer,
to punish a child without explaining their wrong,
or so much more
is to forsake goodness altogether
is to not live up the incredible challenges of faith and trust and patience and love and virtue and grit
that God gives us as our sustenance,
to feed us, purify us,
strengthen us,

and so is to not love ourselves
and so is to not love at all

i don't know

but give selflessly
love ferociously and fiercely,
with the most utter of gentleness and forgiveness,
to have the greatest strength
and the most utmost wisdom
and suffer for each other like the heroes we are,
bravely and fearlessly
then, maybe, our unborn grandchildren
can have grandchildren of their own,
and besieged love and peace will thrive
in a world that stands poisoned to the marrow,
and utterly bankrupt,
and that, if it realizes its bankruptcy,
despite the illusion of hundreds of trillions of dollars,
is to die in nuclear holocaust,
or explode into a world
with miraculous love and intelligent freedom.

sweet idiot wind

10-7-14

Dearest Becca,
For Six years have I madly been in love with you,
ferociously sometimes, kindly and full of warmth other times,
I've cried my guts out to you hundreds of times,
Idiot wind,
Soon, you'll married to some dumb cop, oh he'll keep you safe,
In the end of the world, the safety I always promised
To never keep you safe from, so that you'd grow
Face the world's injustice and turn it to art,
Sweet idiot wind, I expected so much more,
You're sweet and serene rage and glory,
Sweet idiot wind,
Now,
Now you've had a cop call my parents
Because I messaged a friend of yours to ask if it was OK
To, after all these years, see you at last,
Sweet idiot wind,
And you'll never know my rage and my glory,
While the World stands bankrupt and at the end of times,
Sweet idiot wind,
Just hoping for a happy ending that only I could give you,
I've been single for six years, hoping, praying, singing to you, and you only
Spending two weeks out of school, writing you that album,
So painfully heartbroken,
Sweet idiot wind,
Stupid Water-woman with the watery moondream eyes,
Yes, dearest, finally you found the easy way out,
Stupid Water-woman with the watery moondream eyes,
No, you'll never know a man who loves you more than me,
And you've torn me apart in a million ways,
But in the end, I'll have the final laugh,
Because you wanted the end of the game too early,

Yes, I want the happy ending,
But not now, God knows not yet,
So that it'll be truly earned,
And what have you?
Lovely illusion, marrying a cop in a world
Of neo-nazis and police states, and you married a cop....

Congratulations, you have safety at last,
But, dear, I have Life,
So only Time will tell
Just who has fell, and who's been left behind
When you've gone your way and I've gone mine,
Sweet idiot wind...

If I Die Early and Mean

9-6-'15

If I die early, violent and sudden,
Let my compatriots know peace.
Blood in my mouth and in my eyes,
As though my Soul's been fleeced,
If I go, meaningless or mean,
Know that the voyage goes on,
Know that I continue Being.

For my religion is not some random belief,
But rather Truth I know
For my Soul is a traveler
And by Death, what greater joy can unfold?
For I'll be Reborn, and live anew
And my years were ripe with joy.
So let not a moment of ugliness pin me down
inside any mind lost to Time.

No, Happiness is my Soul's gift
and Freedom I eternally Know
So let go with grace and love
and feel me shining in the snow.

Steer The Stars

5-16-'15

Steer the stars around a fine blue sun,
and into a netherworld of a hue,
While sometimes I stare at the fact of evil—
Yet I gotta remember that heaven goes through
through a cloud detesting remorse.

Echoes and ghost-chills,
What a somber fucking moon,
I wanna slither to a new dimension,
They say Scorpio's been a real pain,
But what is horseshit by any other name?

The tales have faded away
and where's my damn bonfire? I Sigh.

Ease a rapid tumbling mountain,
the junctures of a mind's eye
can get so bloody dualistic,
And darkness falls upon the eye of the deep,
Exploding skies and rugged tears,
They're rugged cuz it's acid tears that fall
When you're nowhere near scaling that wall,
And yet been bitten by a fall,
Let my engine stall
And crash in. To. You.

Well, perfection is a distasteful bent,
This bird's a regurgitant,
But when the sun pokes his playful
first beam into the sky,
I'll look you in the eye
And say, "Just help me pick up the pieces."

And the rest is a dust jacket of history
wrapped in coveralls.

suction cup opera

The suction cup opera played a terrible song
As we were lost in the hubbub and yearning for rest,
There is no end to the bloody pap smear,
Yelled Diego above all the rest.
The tinker bell tune wailed out during the torrential gale
And we were frightened in the fog
God said there's no place better than within,
And we went to jack frost's rescue in the smog.

Hold me now closer,
Wizardress of the roiling underworld,
Hold me now dearer,
Princess of the noon-time tide,
Dream me now wholer,
Autumn's sweetest bride,
And the thunderguns sing a higher song
Than Brittany of the deceased,

And it brings peace,
And it brings peace,
Yes, yes it finally does indeed bring peace.

11-18-'15

StarShine Lady

6-11-'15

She skates on water, like glory's first flame,
and dances like an angel, unwinding again,
and kisses the sunrise when she awakens
and falls into bed, giving the world her bliss,

starshine, Madeline,
explosions so serene
starshine on her eyeline,
grooving like the world divine

oceans and acid

10-21-'15

Oceans of rain in my eyes and acid in my mind,
Stomach aflame and I get so sick of my ego's game.
Can't stand my own voice and hardly a boy,
The maniac is me and I sometimes can't see
Through this veil of harsh tooth truth

What a low light is falling on my soul
Wish there was somewhere to go,
But darkness and laser aliens
of weird crutches find me
with a mind that knows what it is
to sin in your thoughts

Find me again, gentle sky
Bath me again, peaceful rain
Kiss me again, lucid water woman,
For now I understand my sin.
So make it alright again.

the river shivers (sadistic beercan)

2-7-14

The ages melt
in the sinking, rising sun of time
awareness comes, like the agonized yet smiling friend
yet when the ego melts
I echo the broiling streetlight
and the sadistic beercan
embracing eternity in a weird moment
that means it all
as the snow falls like nothing matters.

and sometimes,
sometimes i become it all
meaning screams with love
and I'm simply laughing keys
on the keyboard that hears my thoughts
better than I know myself.

I found eternal life
in the thought that the brain is like a radio
and consciousness is an energy it tunes into.
So I'm eternal,
and the river shivers.

Violet Stereo

2-28-'15

sun in my eyes and i'm scouring wild.
nothing left to say or see,
as if there had never been, nor would,
be anything here for me
but liberated humanity...

but the nightlife is coming alive
succulent eyes
and i'm a party-maniac with a level third eye
wondering how and where and never why
yeah, sun in my eyes, and they're glinting.

and the answer is letting thoughts go
& finding yourself, yummy sublime,
letting yourself go
like no fuzziness but slurping wine
and i'm dancing like a cowboy
and stars have blown my mind's eye
vigorous alive,
dancing like a cowboy
and singing like a nectarine on a violet stereo
crunchy guitars and a master meditator
letting go
& coming alive...

when so many things are wrong

11-11-'15

Tough lessons of growing up.
Knowing of innocence and knowing of sin.
Dark dreams and hazy nights,
now I'll breathe that it's alright again.

I've got God but still eat wretched animals' meat,
gotta breathe that it's ok,
cuz i gotta eat and God knows I'm weak
strong like a pterodactyl, weak like
his furry prey,
God, sometimes its' hard
to breathe that it's Ok.

Sin is dark in its violence,
makes the air in the room vanish,
suffocating smoke, and I'm
traveling while broke,
getting a hangover of gnarley energy
out of my sleepy bed-time brain.

And I'm healing again,
because evil is rare though powerful and vast,
but within my heart is a space
with quietly unfurling sails,
and my heart breaks open,
beauty gong, supple song,
wondering how to make it right
when so many things are wrong.

Heart ache, heart break, weeping
through a blurry world of smearing light,
in the hospital, walking down the road,
No, sometimes it just ain't right...

Rise again, puppy dog turned to ferocious Man,
Learn your power, Learn your supremacy, Learn
the supple linguistic interplay of your
nonverbal love, in the ferocity of your affections,
In the gifts you make from a star-filled night life,
dance like you're making love to the Universe,
sway beneath these delicious stars,
And breathe life into your aching bones,

For the sky is alight and these streaming tears
will wash away the scarlet shades of your parlor's
crooked pallor,

And when we meet, I'll awaken you,
For you've been slumbering and wond'ring when,

Well, the sky will open between us, twin lovers,
the seas will part,
and I'll mosey up to you, laughing and laying low,
pull from behind my back a single rose,
and say the words, "It's worth it now.
"It's worth it now."

8-18-'15

Tell me true young baby blue,
How did you melt the snow?
How did you sing
To the world again,
When madness was the truest bling?

Father in the sky never answered Why,
So I trucked onward through the snow.
Father in the sky while pistols pop
And bullets fly,
How can you wonder so?
I catapult so slow.

Treat me warm like you did back home
Tell me answers are here for me,
But young baby blue warmed a solstice true,
And sent color cascading through
Through the town nestled on the hill.

And I'll never know for sure,
But it helps that you're here,
And mountains collapse toward peace.
Tell me true, young baby blue,
How you escaped Pop's eyes' death gaze
and relax, someday to escape
such a haze.

anemic moon and rock explosions

7-16-14

after years without art, here I breathe
my mind turning over thru this surf and pebbly sand
as summer wanes, I feel the frenetic night,
scorching like a sunlit glove in the immense fires
of a life beginning to gain momentum

~I'm beginning to soar, yet all alone~
yes, all alone I am, but soon chiseled...

hours kiss and melt, but my energy returned
in a place of loud alcoholism and quiet,
quiet silence, thru the flames of night
and the pounding rock 'n' roll

Finding myself as laziness is subdued
by the lust for change
sip me down the gizzard of night

rolling thru the suburban and white-collar sprawl
sulfide lights and dog shit, i no longer care,
waging a war against boredom and into flow
tell me where the hours go

the years go by, sliding along rockbeds
and nursed by gentle-cool pools
~Time can grow so inky~
but when the ink settles, the flow continues
sliding down an ancient river
towards more hells and heavens
It's the ancient dream of Life,
while the waves rock against the shore,
and
and this music pulls me somewhere,
call it eternity,
yet the journey continues
and the hippie drummers know the beat.

On The Decline

4-22-14

Helplessly searching
through arboretums of agony,
Tell me it's in retreat,
Tell me I'm finding me.

The songs bind like forgotten wine,
The birds sing like they're here again,
The soul owns this agony,
And my memory has been in retreat...
But now it's on the offensive,
So don't take offense or you'll find it,

Remember that a thousand tears,
began with one sweet kiss,
And remember you're living up
Up to a fallen sun...

Don't let go of the stars, sweet child,
Don't let go of the mercury gaze,
Don't let go of your darkest hours,
Don't let go because it's in the bag,
Haunting not but a naughty soul...

The sun and the stars were where you were free,
So let not this tired song surround you,
For you're past the darkest hours,
Living a life that's gradually turning sublime,
turning into the finest of wine.

Like a long-lost song,
Like an ancient memory,
Like a gloomy moon turned brilliant,
Like the world stopped going wrong...

And you live in this ecstasy of ecstatic decline,
You live in this hay-wire world all the time,
You live like your life will never end,
You live like the joy is coming on again...

So you're a superhero for the joy,
So you're a soul remorselessly trying,
So you're a superhero for the joy,
So sing out, because Death is on the decline,
your spirit's song growing along
turning into the finest of wine.

Bad Stuff Is Temporary

Kiss the Goddess's Eyes, and float away
Was the call we heard them say,
A life of serene meanderings,
Calling up from the fore.

I can't believe that life is these
Unending tired pleas,
So I'll turn up the radio oh so loud,
Watch the face of the sunrise sky
and, in awe, stop besieging my brain with "Why?"

Oh Whiskey, oh my song and my weird dream
my artichoke smoked oddness dream,
never could these constellations so perfectly align
if this wasn't truly our time,
as the saviors of democracy.

Kiss me sweetheart and goodnight
became a barbarous plight
but I know of peace in these raging eddies
and when it's wrong I fall away,
I spell out so much but never know what to say,
so relax into an ocean tide
and bloom, youngest sister,
bloom awake and alive.

8-11-'15

Black and Green

6-6-14

Spring-Time Mist expanding like a growing egg
Leaves are budding in Springtime's golden green,
Take me higher, to a creative dream-time world,
Drift me down this river to bliss.

Don't let me go, don't let me go,
Let me walk and strive and rock and dive
Down a hazy-water's edge to a happy dawn
I'm living and I'm finding my way fin'lly home.

Beat me up and beat me down, it's ok
Don't much care for the fake glossy shine,
Beat me around and take me into a new soul-river
Tell me the answers are falling like a summer's rain.

Tell me the song repeats with every fourth-beat
Tell me these stars live just for me and you,
Tell me the fire burns it's life for us
And let my consciousness coalesce on a dove,
simmering sweet.

Sing me home now, watermelon lady
Sing me home now, the song is exploding
Sing me home now, I'm coming to pieces
in a brand new coalezion to intimacy
simmering sweet.

We'll look back on these days and laugh
It worked out in a tremulous way,
We'll look back on these days and laugh
Because the sky really kicked ass,
All the way.

Chinese New Year

1-18-14

drinking in the wisdom of the ages
beneath a florrid, blurry sun
the pains unwind how the nightmares bind
and I float beneath a timeless spotlight.

sing to me a fairy's song
when we're lost in the woods
and oh-so alone.
sing it to me on a celtic dulcimer
bring to me my ancient home.

the stars burn old light
into my pupils and I quake in sleep
the waves play a dance of the ages
I'm stunned and I'm trembling
surrounded by an angry orchard
and an anguished moon.

I come alive with gentle hand-claps
falling like the rain on cobbled streets.
My engines rev with the silence of
Turkish rain in Egyptian deserts,
and I'm falling down a gushing waterfall
into a Chinese New year
that hums with the burbling brook of progress.

Dear Sex-Slave Masters (A Poem of Cosmic Redemption)
4-10-14

Dear Sex-Slave-Masters, I donate unto you the fires of Hell.
I believe in these now,
they're the power of your hatred turned onto yourself,
as you will do once you die,
supremely, totally, completely.
 No light, no love, for none was in your brain,
Only the power of your domination-style hatred turned
onto itself.

The microcosm of your evil I've seen,
it's like sucking marrow from the bone,
but the bone goes on forever and the marrow is poison.
I feel your hatred, it coarses through my fetted veins,
yet I cry and beat against
against it's power of hatred.
It fucks me up,
it hurts me,
it's hateful and it's evil, and I feel it, and
and, and,
and I damn you unto eternal damnation.
I do not lend you the slightest bit of love,
For you deserve none...

You weren't always this way, you have felt love,
at least one moment of your life, and therein
may lie your salvation,

God always lends a life-line...
If only you can let go of your negativity...
I've glimpsed your domination,
Putting Women and Men through incredible fire and pressure
And jacking them off lovelessly,
How long do you do this to them before you end their lives?
Each moment I breathe,
how many are going through this torment?

You will learn suffering.
You will learn pain.
And God will find you.
Will find you once you've been beaten so low
that the only hope left
Is to succumb to desperation,
desperation so deeply that
you open your soul to God
and find deliverance. Fuck ya.

And on that broken day,
when your hatred has turned against you,
and you have been elevated and it dies beneath you,

I will hold you in my arms,
as you weep in the tremendous
pains of the sins you have performed

And I will say, "Free them." And you will,
They'll be returned home to cry tears of healing joy.
"it's ok, it's over now,"
and you will ask, "How can I forgive myself?"
And I will say, "Turn to the forgiveness and Love of the Christ."
And you will ask "How can I know Christ?"
And I will say, "But open your heart."
And in your agony, you will...
And the rain will fall
in a whirlwind of flowerpetals and angsty remembrances,
and your soul will weep and beg,
and the love will fall like liquid sunlight
and we'll meet one another upon that sunlight shore forgiven,
forgiven forevermore,
and we'll each turn to the task of forgiving more lost Souls,
and the birds will chirp in elation.

Dreaming Slurpid

Slurpidly dreaming, what a vast exaggeration
but no, you never know in a world, so redemption!
Slurpidly dreaming, well, does it even matter the name?
I'm skating down ice into a mountain-gong's refrain.

Insipid yellow is the tongue-beat of the broken class
Insipid yellow, but this flavor's here to last
Insipid yellow, but the chains, they do break loose
Tell me it's tea and promises
Tell me my soul's on the loose,
and outta her noose.

Beauty, perfect, sing your mountain's gong
Now I would be manic, but my medicine peels on,
Beauty, perfect, and the mountain gong's climax
is a release and a quiet breathe, and
and we're in it to the last.

Infinite time, by another name it's fine
Time don't have to be an enemy, if you stick true
to gorgeous clarity,
Hell-bent on tomorrow and it can get ugly
But to believe in that which ain't real...

Excelsior, horrorshow comet-blitz
like tomorrow lands like this
it's ok, it's just a gong of fury
and the world meets it with its mercy

the plantes are breathing hard tonight
to cancel out humanity's weirdest sight
the planets revolve and pulse and sing
and we're getting on the right track, again.

call it music sweet and supply-cool
you know we were meant to land
on this hay-crazed dastardly spiral
and it's ok, baby breath
we're singing aloud again like the sonorous left.

so sing out, baby blue pumpkin true
sing out, it's OK, reverent blue
so sing out, baby blue
we're rocking into a tomorrow chill
and that's all that must be known by you.

so breathe, baby, baby breathe true.

10-21-'15

Forever's Crushing Dawn

2-5-14

graduating from the overly-intellectual crawl
and embracing night-sounds
beneath a burning streetlight
in the balmy green excitement
revving towards dawn cuz nothing's wrong
and when the bacon sizzles with the sunrise
, but a foggy moment later,
I feel all the eternity of my soul,
walk outside and find refuge in the dimming stars
and feel grateful
that when I feel the wisdom to give up
the parachute of life catches me
for a gentle rollercoaster
and a mosey down an ancient lane.

and in these kisses with Eternity,
what do I gain?
A.   Spirit, in a thunderclap
        Spirit, in the moistness of the grass's dew,
        Spirit, in her darling smile's eyes
        Spirit, rushing up from a mesmerizing dawn,
        and the knowledge we're here forever,
forever and on,
that the ride shall never end
and a sun of positivity glows in my chest
before slumber with her hair
and a fable fairy song
bucking in Forever's crushing dawn.

Found my song

9-18-'15

Found my song, in the pines and the wines,
Found my song in summer and snow
A bugle of Zen and feelings ripening again,
Hard to believe the profundity of the answer I've found.

I see a beach and I see the spray,
See the gulls and their madly fray,
I see the future as a multitude of grey,
I see answers and feel the pulse-line,
Echoing through ocean cascades.
The pen scratches so fine.

And I'm gaining fire in my mind and in the crookedly time,
I'm playing beauty truth and cool,
I'm laying low and not too worried
Where I'll go
And the starblasts signal the future,
In the sand, the waves a row,
Beneath the surface,
and atop is
Skating over ice.

Sink the future alight,
Sink me into a mesmerizing time,
Well, it's all here and now, a
Sunburst anyhow,
and the future sinks into here.

cuz zen is so real and it's felt in my fun,
Heaven returned, and I'm being redone...

If all the world knew what I know
We'd be in Heaven tonight.
I really can't give too much cred
to dystopia so bad,
Tho if everyone felt my lows, we'd regress a thousand years
But that's an impossibility,
And Hell falls away to memories,
So fine.

But I've constructed a bridge over my canyon,
And one over my moat,
Goodness true serene ocean blue,
And a dreamsong finds me,

Blessings befall me,
and beauty washes through,
and wondering where and how you are,
Sweet lady blue.

The violin ushers in the orgasmic end,
Crescendo of mad fury and succulent flame,
The drums rattle and roll,
The chg chg of a muted guitar,
And enter star world,
Water sliding through words
But what's real to me is a full stomach,
A wailing guitarist with barbershopesque jingles,
A beer being savoured,
And a sun setting while a clock chimes,

And it's all feelings. Cuz I won the game
And the rest is lingerie and laughter.

Free As The Sky Is Wide

8-21-'15

Being in being inside love,
envelop me from the heart.
Sky sun slinks low
and here we go,
Slinking groovy cool.

Open myself to artistry,
Master chisel it intimately
Bend it around a world's goofy idiocy,
And write it valid real.
And *play it sweetness song*
alive...

Tell me I'm alive for a reason,
tell it in my heart,
She's beauty true and cool too,
Massage it cool blue and singing thru
A world on a high-wire beam,
T'is glory to watch her dream,
Bubbly serene,
Around a green sunbeam.

And life wiggles,
On the Earth's rugged soil,
Lambasting those who beauty recoil,
Standing on the asphalt and laugh;
Free as the sky is wide.

Grungy Tenement in Heaven

6-19-'15

Lucky skies and fallen eyes,
here's a kiss for your despair
Memories alight, laughing on an exquisite night,
the pain a test, so try loose, not uptight
let the drums crash and roll

i met you in the corners, in the darkest of the divine
i dug your agonized laughter, it was like a monument of helter skelter
and when up came the black stuff, brought on by my LSA
you laughed so we wouldn't cry and told me
"God has one hell of a sense of humor,"
and we laughed in the cool night air.

The stars never shined so brightly as they did
The day before you died,
The snow never fell so hard
the moment your pitter-patter heart ceased,
and the sunset never felt so final,
nor the next sunrise so complete
when they read your will and I received
your Bukowski-esque book of tainted poetry,
and I could find your piss-and-vinegar personality
whenever your callous inglory was needed,

so let the jukebox play one more sad Gaelic tune,
and I'll down this whiskey like you,
stumble into bed and come to
knowing your blessings of crooked humor await me
in some grungy tenement in heaven.

Hot-Air Balloons

7-16-14

The night came on like a blast of thunder,
We looked at each other and we grinned
cuz the night arrived before the dusk
and when morning comes, we'll ride
into a sacred, melting sun of purest gold,
and expectations are hot-air balloons in my heart.

We'll ride out of this paranoid town for waters
that glimmer like liquid love,
riding past the small towns that hold such anger,
we'll ride into the multicultural city,
and when the jazzmen lilt and tumble and scream,
We'll laugh, cuz now
expectations are like hot-air balloons in my heart
and I'm soaring.

Freedom found me in the death-valley of women's touch,
in text that oozes and flows,
and emotion-typing suffused with intelligent meanderings
bring me back to my heightened realm
and when we meet atop the pyramid of intelligent   achievement
and on the breast of the ocean of artistic magnificence
we'll laugh as the stars fall down around us,
clothed in the love of one another,
and laughing above the bedrock,
for we've made it to a higher slumber and silly   awakeness,
and the engine hums,
while hope is hot-air balloons in my heart.

.

The infinity of a white wall's potential,
The beauty of sullen rain's emotion,
The mesmerizing truth of just knowing
That the negative is being sent away.

Infinite Imagination's Rebirth

2-18-'15

Trying, oh I'm trying, to find my grooviest way...
maybe it's that I'm not ganja-ing but I had never had to
in the olden times, and I know
oh woah woah, it can be hell for me, such a fucking pity.
So I'm trying just to fathom how to do it all and be at peace,
How to keep the sun's rays a mellow sheen,
How to dance with the flow, to live, let live, let it flow,
And only humbly to know...
cuz it's a bitch to be a kid and more to be grown,
and I wonder where this flow will go...

Sail me on the curvy sea, sing me a dream
and dreamtime a melody to me,
Tell me the summer sun's song will never go wholly out or away,
For we rest in timelessness and, as such, all is real and true, truly
All is here, all now, and imagination is real...

Real for one and two, me and you and you,
yes, to see it at last that being an artist is not something we do,
but rather, that

Truth is and isn't subjective, but...
my personal truth can be and is
what I wish her to be, so long as i'm good,
~and i am good~

and protect myself, do not accept the crooked notion
that the negative applies to me...
just as Christ died to redeem us, so he frees us,
for so it is that we are free...

And in this innocence lay a quiet light, within which we are found,
suffused with the wisdom of the ages, or at least,
at least the ages themselves,
so we are free to dance and sing and make merry,
in our rabbit hole, in our den, with our magic, and timeless insight,
for now the real is ours,
and ours is the splendid sunrise of the soul.

little stars and little prayers a go-go

1-11-15

little stars and little prayers,
in a little girl's eyes,
so precious are these gentle whispers
so precious are these reverent times

indigo the dyes a go-go
who knows when we're lost, where we go
but in our own heartcave
is the treasures of life,
the bounty of Christ,
all alight,
all a dazzle,
all a go-go....

forgotten incense, she lingers
like a tired boy's eyes
and complications can rule and scream
but raise your arms and surrender
to gentle crying and gentle peace,

as the snowflakes fall so gently,
as the clock ticks a long lost age's key,
as the beauty of loss and the loss of beauty
swirls through the pretty We,

humility is innocence,
and innocence is a quiet smile,
the silence of the pre-dawn morning
and the heart is a hearth
that begs to warm us all....

Living Profound

Living in a profound way, energies crashing,
serene meaning,
Profound Freedom, engines screaming,
Tell me of a lightsource that's heavy with dance-o-hol, like
Liquid thunder, tell it to me true, the ocean a watery blue,
Tell me we can sweep ourselves off our feet, and rush
with ebony lava-flows and oh, the places we'll go?
and meet with righteous saturation, skim-boarding stellar
like cosmic energies that sing and dance-supremacy melting,
and tell me if these eye-kick thunderwash images and curlicue metaphors
can return us to a place of organic hearth-flame and crushing
crushing icecubes frozen from boiling and turquoise
sunlight flushing through like orange-juice and jiving...
tell it to me, liquid blue,
tell it to me true...

Jan 27, 2015 C.E.

Markus Means/Jesus' Joke/but roll

2-8-'15

Markus means, with a cherry on top
please let sensuality find me...
Sex on the summer night's beach,
'Neath stars that purr like a pearly oyster's tune
Oh let Markus mean,
Let this imagination sing delirious but delicious
Time-capsules of a once-forgotten faith
Let love be found like the cool summer wind,
Oh let Markus means,
Let my meaning and meaningfulness be my own,
To share with the lucky few,
Let me see skyscrapers, and see hope and genius
Knowing also of the workerman's fall
From grace we come and may us with she be,
Like a tired lament of an ancient eternity,
Let beauty flush on her rosy cheeks,

please wing/sing my story to me...

Yes feelings, yes lucid watery mind,
Yes feelings be not of the extreme,
But the gorgeousness in this truth,
To my beatnicked ocean-Cry! Cry my dearest, cry cry
I'll cry my dearness,
Let in not the chains to be seen,
Don't take without a grain of humor that perfect
    Perfect beings can be sinners in the best of ways,
Jesus' joke, for the ages to be,
Feel the den of love
As the night sings in quiet soliloquy,
Let the night in, darling son,
Let beauty reward be,
So sing me a song, my feelings
And may the same be for thee,
Type-writer reader audience We, audience Me,
Lyricality in subjectivity,
Let the drum songs not ever disagree;

but *roll*.

Masterpiece Crescendo 1 & 2

Stars in tune and I am my guitar, the twinkling notes and purple rhythms,
Stars in tune and I dance through and through, because I know a secret
one of beauty and delicious intrigue
which I beg you to pardon me for spilling
but I do believe in magic, magical intelligence,
like not a weapon but like a soundwave that invades and
      instills peace,
because I'd rather be Ted from Bill & Ted than Jesus, the sweet one,
but my teenage soul is snappin' with these keys
and what I wish most to express is that imagination is real,
which is why it's called "Is-Rael," or The Holy Land,
and that fusion between the twin hemispheres of the brain   is
that fuzion IS imagination, and
writing and music and expression through the arts
is training for situations and Holy Reverence and if the energy is light enough
Intense Sunrise Mellow with Tangerine,
the teenager then comes out, and the play is fantastical,
rest now, sweet one,
Rest in play,
Thine race be won, and gentle arms of glory be thine   ~smile dawn~
alive like perfection...

      cuz
I discovered the living breathing Soul of Spirit that is   God
I discovered it when I found that Life and Positivity are
      Inside Me,
& that I am a lightsaber of Positivity through the fun I embody,
because I found the literal keys to freedom,
and they crack and they sparkle on this typewriter, baby,
      baby oh they do,
and the real true key to positivity is a cool Jedi's lightsaber
a life-giving tool,
and in the awesomeness of lightsabers and my real and true knowledge
of the Force, the Living God,
the inventiveness of being a clear blue artist dood,
flushing like a blushing bumblebee,
flushing like an iris enlarged in rosy merriment,
so cowabunga calls, I feel it passion dragonfruit,
and the sun sings me home, cool dance

because all i need to know
is Positivity is something that's been Proven, even by me,
and so We've got this one.
we just have to know that we know the Holy Open Secret.

Jan. 27, 2015

mesmerizing Timeless cascades:

4-16-14

silly putty crashing on a claymation shore,
rev the engines one tired last time,
and the stars, surrounded by trees, are peering in,

and the trees are turpentine factories,
and the trees are gin factories,
yet their branches speak of Indian majesty,
speak written language sloshing with fire in the Sol-Light,
of early morning at flaming dawn,
and sacred fire drips from the dewy leaves,

and I'm standing naked in the face of Eternity,
I'm standing naked for a UFO to beam me into the nether-regions of Time,
I'm standing naked to be displaced for a twirl through the cosmos,
and a moment later returned to the smell of incense and mango-scented candles,
knowing it's but Eight A.M.

My Brother, I Wonder

9-18-'15

My brother, I wonder at how we're the same song,
As I watch *Hackers* (the movie)
Sip beer, vape, and write to a world of
The reverent silence of eternity,

You need meaning, boy cowabunga,
Your sun sinks so low.
I wish I could give you writing and genius,
They lay dormant in your DNA
But you don't open the passage and the package,
For fear of the word 'Gay.'

I'd curse if I could,
It puts a sour taste in my mouth,
And frustration screams up
Like a volcano of tepid dust,
And it tastes like I'll never know why
You were too afraid to fly.

my soul's song of love

2-13-14

supplestar, she's my supplestar,
diamonds in her coffee eyes,
heart ever on the line,
she's my diamond honey-bun,
she's my soul,
she's the softness of beauty,
and her expression...

the word "love" can not express
how i feel when i see her gentle eyes,
and through them glimpse the beauty of her emotion,
her laughter sweeter than nectar,
her soul so young, so innocent,
and my heart-cave billows
as the prairie brushfire of a thousand years
sings to me of my soul's biblical song...

mystery's door

2-10-'15

sometimes i think i don't deserve, yea
embers of a fallen sea
underwater volcanoes with a twist of rum
slamming oceanspray back to me

i look out over these waters, these tides
waves roiling and crashing against
against a sunlit shore
once i would have sang i know it all
now i'm downfounded as never i knew at all before.

when the moon is blood red
and the snow a poignant blue
i'll know i'm just a passenger
not the DJ of these hues.

sometimes i wonder where went my star
to what places do the ghosts of morning doves go?
now i'll only know myself
and leave open mystery's door.

onward

12-16-'15

she sang like miracles,
the summer sun was remorseless in her vision. but it held the promises of the future.
a room bathed in golden light, a cool room, and purple   dashed paint
swimming in on the floor, laughing in frenzied mania   disease,
yes, the beauty delves, gentle soar, the beauty delves
through the floor into a sci-fi world of tomorrow
where we clang through cyberpunk taxi to the monitor   glow,
and heaven becomes a monumentous moment alive,

and at the pool with turkish jade tiles, we swam in a warm pool and
we discussed maroon tides in the bayous,
wondering aloud if the answers weren't in our keys
and where our keys were, and if it weren't all a blasphemy to not go looking
digging into the recesses of our minds
to find if we knew maybe someone who spoke the answers   once,
so we shook hands, and we scoured wild.

a decade later and ben dug in and sold out,
monica ran away and lost her soul,
jessica, that precious gem, she lost her mind in the cocaine halls and sucking balls,
alexis blew her brains out on pills and died, and there was the rumor that guy fucked her in the mortuary,
and you didn't sell out but turned colder, and i look to myself now,
shining bodhisattva of a distant realm,
and the answer is alive,
like the rolling highway road,
the answer is alive, and onward
onward my vehicle feet roll.

ouroboric

1-21-'15

in a new millenium hitting the '15's, such laughing melodiciously.

the sky wilts under these preposterous heinouses,
but hope grows its roots still more deeply,
and the molecules of slavery are crunched
and processes through the miracules of freedom,

the world breathes,
the world breathes,
and the ancient, my ancient
my ancient celebration of the human condition
she/he heals, dastardly squigglard,
and a laugh at the cosmic conditions,

well, so i lose knowing
well, so i lose what i had thought
was fundamental to my brain-ing
well, so depth is this lovely child's innocence,
well, so we found ourselves again,

and i grin
rock-solid rock music of
of oh, oh i grin

cuz i had peace of mind and i rocked it
i had peace of mind and i blew it
i have peace of mind and i rock it
turpentile and squiggly-huge,
my big crunches into little,
my little exacer-evolves into bigger
sillbe putty of a sillbe nation,
what can we still-be?

the honor is a depth-defying squiggle-crunch
and honor is the spirit of Gold yang's self,

well, this may all seem incoherent,
but not-knowing is so much of feeling,
and without feeling we are un-centered and ungrounded,
let the whale-call vorble,
and i'm a singeing lasagna
on the brown-cheese grill
of a world ripening to pizza-yum...

Pharaoh Dance

Sluggish morning and fire-hot winter's day
body burning like a firework
Christmas eggnog and adorning myself
In the armor of Christ
It's a beautiful soul in my heart.

Pharaoh dance and ancient sand blowing
The window to the past
My soul is ancient and profound and ripe
And I'm excelling at last.

Praise the mountains and praise the streams
Praise her heart and praise the sea
The answers rain down, so gently on me,
And a heavencusp ascends like the gentle sway,
Of her stroll down ivy lane beneath a tremendous rainbow...

Pharaoh Dance,
On a beautifully-lit way.

Portal Soul

growing the fuck up around a blistering sun,
warping itself into my goofystupid brain,

sing for me the last notes of an arabian tragedy
put to delectable song,
tell me the song is in my soul and give me whiskey
and my beard will sing it plainly home...

my God, I'm finding masculinity,
and my brother went through hospitals for me
trying to demonstrate what was wrong
that i may singe at the edges.
now i grasp into the darkroom,
and heaven pulls me so strongly home...

been a while, Lord has it been a while
since castles and knightly heroes called my name,
every action movie ended in stupid couldn't-feel,
and my soul turned to mush and steel,
and acid tears melted the mush away
and my soul was skeleton and gray.

but light a happy call through your heart-beat's trombone,
Lord has the light awakened again, and I'm smearing
smearing into the liquid gel sea,
tangerine-turquoise haze all night and day,
but honey, we're living, and this delicious mind,
Lord, the hard stuff is *melting*
melting into sane liquid pudding,
melting away.

Tell me I'm here again and it's cool,
cuz my genius is coming on again,
and Jesus' love is liquid Gold and I'm a pisces fish
flowing through eternity into you,
divine woman awaiting divination,
liquid blue, seeping through,
into a mesmerizing song,
and the acid melted many a tear,
but Lordesse, we're dancing here,
down through the ages, into wine,

Lordesse, we're dancing,
dancing, dancing, and dancing
dancing forever and on again,
Liquid blue, me and you,
so let your trombone heart sear through the ages,
and we're home again....

3-20-14

Rocking in the Heart

2-14

Rocking cuz the sun's been sinking,

Rocking cuz my heart's a flame

Rocking cuz the world's new, yet ancient

Rocking cuz it's comin' on new again.

Ancient slumbers beg for release

into the stars of lightning-bugs

lifting into the sky

ancient slumbers beg for release

and I'm alive again,

raising the flag of today.

beneath a streetlamp, my spirit soars

celebrating an ancient game,

an ancient game and it's life again

Rocking cuz it's comin' on again.

Starlight, ancient and starlight new,

bring me peace and something true

Starlight, ancient and starlight new

Come to me in a kiss

I'll wrap you up and never miss

touching you in the tenderness of the heart.

rolling jelly

6-24-14

succulent waters that look like rolling jelly,
the world breathes an incense ode,
her heart is beating, her eyes wide with idealism,
she brushes through the door and looks up
into an open nighttime sky
in which the stars will never set
and she says, to God and a sleeping world,
"Let's crank up the faucet on our Dreams."

Worlds unite in a cascade of water down the falls,
beneath which they've laughed and played so many times
just never together,
but two hearts that beat as one
pulls them through a blurry field towards one another
and when they meet, her gliggling, him smireling,
God answers, saying simply
"Welcome to the life you've earned."

And the stars explode in fireworks
that only the two dreamers can see,
yet they feel a world's emotions
in the mist of the shower door,
and the tinkling of rain on a tin roof--
just as they always have--
except now they feel Life together.

The Joyous Answer (2)

9-28-14 & 10-2/3/4-14

We need not hurt,
nor anger, nor cynicism
but joy, for all the world to see,
dance a dance and love it all...

for eleven years i have battled
with my conscience on whether it is cowardly
to live a fairytale in a world of suffering...
BUT
in my fairytale, I remember what is right
and true and good,
I remember the answer of love and joy
artistry streaming through the clouds,
and that's what everyone loves from me,
not my questioning, but my embrace
and celebration of the human condition
in all its glory and infamy,
beauty and villainy,
for I'm not in the world, nor of it,
but a witness...except
even in witnessing can be pain
and so, the pièce de résistance,
the glorious answer, is--

lol, just in the writing of that, a woman gave me a car, and we drank some...

eat well, sleep well, forgive all, dance, play,
give mirth, face your fears,
love the sinner, forgive the sin...

and my vision, my creative vision
is the only answer for me,
fueled by strength and love and; dignity
rocking on the soil of Earth...

yet the Witness is so much more profound
than a person dumbly watching another get murdered;
no, the Witness is the source of creativity,
for the Witness is the place of safety,
the haven from the storm,
upon which we can watch God's manifestations form,
and be released from the direness of the heartache,
a temple, a safe haven,
even in the midst of the crackling bombs and smashing kneecaps,

where faith can grow like moss onto wet stones in the river,
and, in the brilliance of safety, we can love the drama
with grooviness above clarity,
safety great, yet below; sacred clarity,
and in this place of utmost safety,
the feelings envelop, coalesce, transcend--
and all this, i find in my tales,
in stories, in the wisdom of songs,
in art and dance and making out,
push and contract darling, push and contract,
for in the creation do we understand God,
and most manifest Her brilliance and light.

Sacrificial Columns

9-1-14

Grooving like a minster wheel,
the sun burning and bringing out hallucinations,
the sun slapping me like a red-hot mallet
t'isn't easy being great, but count the blessings
that now are innumerous
and the sky melts, fuscia through the mountains
soaring, diving, driving
into a new life, cosmically-solid
tender as a slipping teat

letting go of a narrow channel
& finding the ocean
sacrificial columns had
surgical pummels
but i'm
drifting into a universe of love.

SunThruJoyousTears Images

6-11-'15

Moonlight massage
like the stiletto woman's corsage,
and the world buckles low.
Honey and a flame
on fire in my mane,
and I breathe profundity's song.

and pain I crunch
like the Kali Goddess's bonemeal lunch,
and step off this girder again.

The trees are the flame,
the sorry sky weeps her pain,
and I'm galloping into a future release
down on my pious knees
but God echoes my inner smile
Maharaji reorients my broken Akashic file,
And the sunrise is the crescendo of awakening.

somewhere in snapping keys

All is calm and all is quiet,
So said the gingerbread man...
But I can see the scowl, the heartache and the fouls,
Burning down a man, a man made of sand.

But to glass he turns, and his soul is reborn,
like a corporeal sea,
An ancient moonlit tide, blinded from my eyes,
And sometimes I don't know how to see,
Just comma to me,
      succulent energy

all is calm and all is serene, somewhere
somewhere in these snapping keys.

splendid excellence chiseling dance

nightline sunset smear, tangerine and flaming
mixed up with bliss on a ride to a sacred Heaven that is orange and black excellence, in a jade chalice
we're beaming, darling precious, and my heart putter putters to a delicious poly-rhythmic celebration, a kiss from the stars
and our minds' eyes swirl in violet and gold, while our heart-lights shine in copper and green
splendid fireworks crackle and we look to our space ship and let out a happy gasp into a delicious sigh, for the universe is open to liquid excellence, amen amen and amen, let's dance like lightning
and we tremble as love approaches

Staring Out

Staring out, over the sea
from a traveling vessel, wondering what be
ahead in the turvid rapid waters,
that oil and boil, coalesce
and breathe out great flame...

you wonder at the game.
you wonder at the nightmares
you wonder of the ocean
and the dreams of the fish in the sea.

it's hard to believe in the rugged lands
what dreams may come, what realities banned
it's hard to believe it's a cohesive whole
but God is mighty, you say while the ocean rolls

Staring out, over the sea
The crew sings ancient tales,
and you wonder what may be
Imagination on fire in the afternoon sun
You wonder where it'll have gone
once all the plays are done.

you wonder till it's only sun
slumbers like magic when the day is done
you wonder if life is truly this song
you wonder, you wonder
until your wonderings are done.

Zen comes like a stolid flame
Zen comes and you know this game,
Beauty caresses around each bend
you wonder, you wonder,
and Zen is gone again.

Staring out, over the sea
You spot land, but with melancholy
The folks all want to land, so they heave ho
pull out the paddles, and inward you go
You wonder what you're about to find
and hope it'll be more than human grime.

Starry night and icebergs alive
You land and meet a raven so wise
Then the natives appear and ask for trades
you teach you learn, the melancholy fades

And in the treasure that profit provides
the people are happy, no fear of sunken tides
You lucked out this time, young samwise green
and the people made home
where there was only sickly green.

9-26-'15

Starry Skies, Momma's Eyes

Starry skies, my Mother's eyes,
The gentle wheeze of the Big Blue Van,
Starry skies, my Momma's eyes,
On a road trip with a plan.

Growing up on the road and at night,
Dadda's music playing slow and soft,
Growing up on the windy road at dawn,
Sunrise in the palm of God.

Starry skies, my Mother's eyes,
Times I cherish as the miles pass by,
Starry skies, my Momma's eyes,
Going to Nana's home again.

2-19-2014

stars and balls and happy monkeys

6-11-14

stars and balls to the wall and i'm laughing
found something that feels like victory,
a happy beginning and closure too,
whew, i blew out my siren flames
just a moment ago
and the world tumbles off my shoulders
and she rolls.

scalliwag and princess bird,
daisies and pecan pies and summer rains,
holy God did I get myself smart,
so, despite evidence to the contrary,
that quest went well
so suckle up the spazming fireworks
let these teeny flames fall upon us
and let's make love beneath a
a furious star fire
as the Milky Way twinkles to us remembrances
cascaded from before time began
when we were more naked more innocent
and chattering--Oh the birds we were!--
and now we've been so much more (& less)
but this appreciation is a splendid book
dancing in the rodeo dustfire
for though these people are idiots,
they're pacified by this country-pop
and therein be safety enough,
so tumble down these towers and walls,
because my truth is burgeoning
and our children shall sing
in God's transcendental freedom
so the stars align
and the monkeys sing their song,
calling us home, happy monkeys
to the Tibetan man's gong.

About the Author:

Brett Harrison has been writing poetry since he was 15 in 2002, and writing stories for years before that. His current published works include *Our Tired Paris Cliché*, *Forgotten Incense*, *Schizm*, and *Electric Water*, all of which are poetry collections. He had prepared another poetry book, *Beatnik*, which is yet to be published. He is working on a short-story collection entitled *Snap! Crackle! breathe...*, as well as a comedy-science fiction book *Colony Number One* with Erik Karsama, an as-yet unnamed children's book with Kimberly Newman, a science-fiction epic named *The Struggle For Transcendence*, and perhaps most significantly, *The Mighty Pen: The Incredible Untold Story of Johnny Passion*. His hobbies include photography, going on walks, bicycling, socializing, and music.

Made in the USA
Columbia, SC
12 January 2018